NFL RIVALRIES

EAGLES VS. GIANTS

By Carrie Myers

Kaleidoscope
Minneapolis, MN

Your Front Row Seat to the Games

This edition first published in 2020 by Kaleidoscope Publishing, Inc.

For information regarding permission, write to
Kaleidoscope Publishing, Inc.
6012 Blue Circle Drive
Minnetonka, MN 55343

Library of Congress Control Number
2019939217

ISBN
978-1-64519-081-3 (library bound)
978-1-64494-166-9 (paperback)
978-1-64519-182-7 (ebook)

Printed in the United States of America.

TABLE OF CONTENTS

CHAPTER 1

A Miraculous Finish

Clouds fill the sky. The air is icy cold. It's perfect weather for another hard-fought game between the Philadelphia Eagles and the New York Giants. Their games are always fierce. But this one, on December 19, 2010, is special.

The teams run onto the field. More than 80,000 fans cheer. It's the rivals' first meeting at the Giants' new stadium. Both teams have playoff hopes, too.

Quarterback Eli Manning gets the Giants started. He passes to Mario Manningham. The receiver scores a 35-yard touchdown. And the Giants keep going. By halftime, they lead 24–3.

The Giants' stadium, now called MetLife Stadium, is located in an area of New Jersey called the Meadowlands.

The Giants' Mario Manningham crosses into the end zone for a touchdown.

Everything is looking good for the Giants. Fans are ready to celebrate a win. But with less than eight minutes left, the Eagles rally. Quarterback Michael Vick passes. Tight end Brent Celek catches it. Then he breaks free. Celek runs into the end zone for a 65-yard touchdown. Two minutes go by. Vick scores again. This time he runs the ball in. Now the Eagles trail just 31–24. And they're not done.

The Eagles stop the Giants. Vick takes over. They have 88 yards to go. Eight plays later, Vick passes the ball. Wide receiver Jeremy Maclin catches it. Touchdown! Now the teams are tied. Only 1:24 remains.

Eagles quarterback Michael Vick passed for 242 yards against the Giants.

HEAD TO HEAD

STATS

Through the 2018 season

EAGLES		GIANTS
84	WINS*	84
50	WINNING PERCENTAGE	50
3251	POINTS SCORED	3297
2	PLAYOFF WINS	2
12 (1975-81)	LONGEST WIN STREAK	(1997-01) 9
4	TOTAL SUPER BOWL VICTORIES	1

* The teams have also played to two ties

DeSean Jackson races into the end zone to secure the Eagles' win.

New York soon faces fourth down. Giants coach Tom Coughlin talks to punter Matt Dodge. He tells Dodge to punt the ball out of bounds. Dodge doesn't. The Eagles' DeSean Jackson almost drops the ball. But he holds on. Then he runs 65 yards. The clock hits zero. But Jackson is in the end zone. It's another touchdown! The Eagles win 38–31.

It was a historic win. The Eagles scored 28 points in less than eight minutes. They also won on a punt return for a touchdown on the last play of **regulation** time. That had never happened in National Football League (NFL) history.

The Eagles–Giants rivalry has had many great moments. This isn't the first. And it isn't the last. There are many more to come.

FUN FACT

In 2013, NFL.com readers voted Jackson's touchdown as the best play of all time.

CHAPTER 2

All Tied Up

The Eagles hardly stood a chance. They were a brand new team in 1933. Their first game was on the road. And they had to face the Giants. New York had already been around for eight seasons. That experience quickly showed.

The teams met at the Polo Grounds in New York. Approximately 18,000 fans watched.

FUN FACT

Only three NFL teams are older than the Giants. They are the Bears, Cardinals, and Packers.

The home team put on quite the show for them. The Giants scored three touchdowns in the first quarter. In the end they won 56–0. It was not the start Philadelphia fans had hoped for. But the Eagles would have more opportunities. The cities are less than 100 miles (161 km) apart. And these two teams would meet many more times.

The Giants and Eagles meet for the second time ever in December 1933.

It was November 20, 1960. The Eagles led 17–10. But the Giants had a chance to tie. Quarterback George Shaw threw to **halfback** Frank Gifford. The Eagles' Chuck Bednarik was right there. He hit Gifford hard, knocking him out.

Gifford later called it "a clean shot." But the play injured his head badly. Plus, Gifford lost the ball. The Eagles took control. They eventually won the game. Later they won the championship, too. Giants fans are still mad about "The Hit."

The Eagles' Chuck Bednarik (60) looks on as Frank Gifford lays on the ground.

MIRACLE AT THE MEADOWLANDS

In 1978, the Giants led the Eagles by five. Only twenty seconds remained. Giants quarterback Joe Pisarcik could end the game. All he needed to do was put his knee down. Instead he tried handing off the ball. **Fullback** Larry Csonka never got control. The ball popped out. Eagles **cornerback** Herm Edwards was right there. "I've gotta get it on the first bounce," he thought. And he did. He ran 26 yards. It was a touchdown! The Eagles won 19–17.

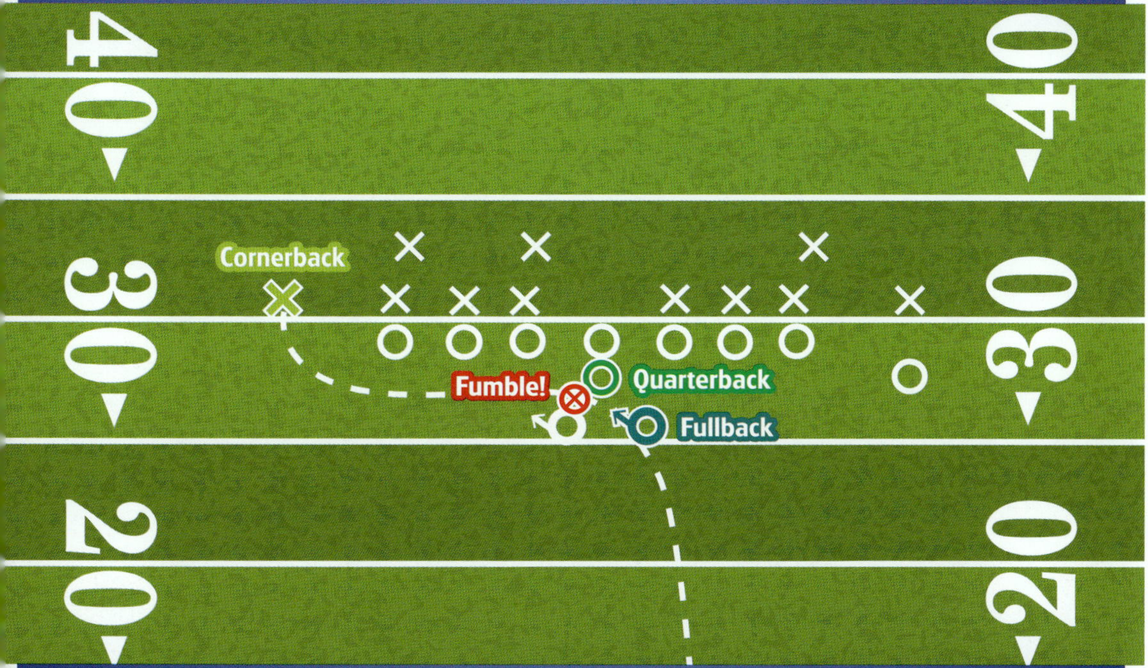

Cornerback: Herm Edwards

Quarterback: Joe Pisarcik

Fullback: Larry Csonka

The Eagles and Giants are often among the top teams in their division.

It's December 27, 1981. The Giants are underdogs. They haven't made the playoffs since 1963. The Eagles, meanwhile, are strong. They played in the Super Bowl the year before. But the Giants surprise everyone. They are soon 20 points ahead. The Eagles score a few times. But they can't come back. The Giants win 27–21. The Eagles go downhill. They don't have another winning record until 1988.

FUN FACT

The NFL Network ranked the Eagles–Giants rivalry as the sixth best of all time.

Another turning point came thirty years later. The Giants had always had a better record against the Eagles. But in the 2010s, the Eagles were catching up. On November 25, 2018, they finally did. The Eagles beat the Giants that day. For the first time ever, the teams were tied. Both teams had 86 wins, 86 losses, and two ties against the other.

CHAPTER 3

Great Rivalry, Great Players

Giants **linebacker** Lawrence Taylor has a target. It's Eagles quarterback Ron Jaworski. Taylor is looking for a **sack**.

Taylor is 6 feet, 3 inches (1.9 m). He weighs 237 pounds (108 kg). Yet he is still super fast. And he can jump. Taylor leaps up. He sails over Eagles running back Keith Byars. He slams Jaworski from behind. Jaworski goes down. He never saw Taylor coming.

Taylor debuted in 1981. He retired in 1993. Only one player had more sacks at the time. Taylor sacked Jaworski 12.5 times. He got Eagles quarterback Randall Cunningham that many times, too.

FUN FACT
In 1989, Eagles quarterback Randall Cunningham was called on to punt against the Giants. His 91-yard punt was the fourth longest in NFL history.

Lawrence Taylor (56) wraps up Eagles quarterback Randall Cunningham.

Eli Manning, left, and Donovan McNabb made sure their teams were contenders.

From 1988 to 1990, the Eagles dominated the Giants. They won five of six matchups. In 1990, the Giants started strong. They had a 10–0 record. But the Eagles ruined it. They crushed the Giants. The score was 31–13.

In 2000, the Eagles–Giants rivalry heated up. *Bleacher Report* called it "The Rivalry of the Decade." Quarterback Donovan McNabb led the Eagles. He led the 2004 Eagles to the Super Bowl. Four other Eagles teams fell one game short of the big game. Quarterback Eli Manning joined the Giants in 2004. He led the 2007 and 2011 Giants to Super Bowl wins.

THE WINNINGEST COACHES

Steve Owen coached the Giants from 1930 to 1953. During his time, they won 153 games out of 270. They won the NFL championship twice. Owen's teams played before the Super Bowl was founded. Andy Reid coached the Eagles from 1999 to 2012. His record was 130 wins out of 224 games. The 2004 Eagles reached the Super Bowl.

Michael Strahan was a Giants **defensive end**. Jon Runyan was an Eagles offensive tackle. They became rivals. In 2001, Strahan set an NFL record. He had 22.5 sacks. Of those, 5.5 were against Runyan and the Eagles. Their battles were tough on the field. But Runyan and Strahan later became friends.

It was October 22, 2001. The Giants were defending conference champions. The Eagles had lost eight straight games to them. Now the Giants tried to make it nine.

The Giants led 9–0 at halftime. All their points came from field goals. Finally, the fourth quarter came. McNabb passed to wide receiver James Thrash. Thrash scored the game's only touchdown. The Eagles won 10–9. This game turned the Eagles around. They played in the next four conference championship games. And they beat the Giants six of the next seven times.

FUN FACT

After his football career, Michael Strahan became a famous broadcaster, including on *Good Morning America*.

Michael Strahan recorded 141.5 sacks in his 15 seasons with the Giants.

CHAPTER 4

Zak DeOssie wasn't going to let the Eagles fans intimidate him.

Superfans, Snowballs, and Santa Claus

Zak DeOssie joined the Giants in 2007. His father, Steve, had played for the Giants, too. So Zak knew what to expect. He was warming up. He would soon be facing the Eagles for the first time. An Eagles fan saw him. The fan insulted DeOssie and his father. He said they were "bums." But DeOssie insulted the fan back. They both laughed.

Eagles fans aren't known for being polite. They boo Giants players. Many Giants players don't mind. They like to be disliked. Former linebacker Spencer Paysinger says, "It makes it fun."

GREASY EAGLES

Eagles fans sometimes celebrate by climbing light poles. In February 2018, the Eagles reached the Super Bowl. The city of Philadelphia didn't want the fans to climb the poles. So the city greased all the light poles. In the Super Bowl, the Eagles beat the New England Patriots. Fans climbed the poles anyway.

Passionate Eagles fans celebrate at the team's Super Bowl parade.

FUN FACT

Embracing their "underdog" status, Eagles fans wore dog masks during the 2017 Super Bowl season.

Philadelphia fans sometimes go too far. Eagles fans have fought in the bleachers. They have thrown objects onto the field. They have thrown bottles and cheesesteaks. In 1968, they even threw snowballs at Santa Claus! But they love their Eagles.

Giants fans wear team colors everywhere. They wear team jerseys. They paint their faces blue and red. They wave blue and red pom-poms. They wear team hats. New York is the biggest city in the United States. People there have lots of entertainment options. But they love the Giants.

New York has a tradition. When a team wins a championship, the city throws a **ticker tape parade**. Thousands of fans line up along Broadway. Many more watch from buildings. Then the team arrives. The players ride on floats. Fans throw confetti out the windows.

The 2011 Giants won the Super Bowl. The city threw a parade. Afterward, the team went to City Hall. The mayor held a ceremony. The team finished at MetLife Stadium. They held a rally. Approximately 40,000 fans showed up.

Eagles and Giants fans have lots to celebrate. Their teams are closely matched. The rivalry is going strong.

FUN FACT

Ticker tape parades leave a big mess. In 2008, more than 300 workers had to clean up the paper!

The Super Bowl champion Giants take part in a ticker tape parade in February 2012.

Rivalry Map

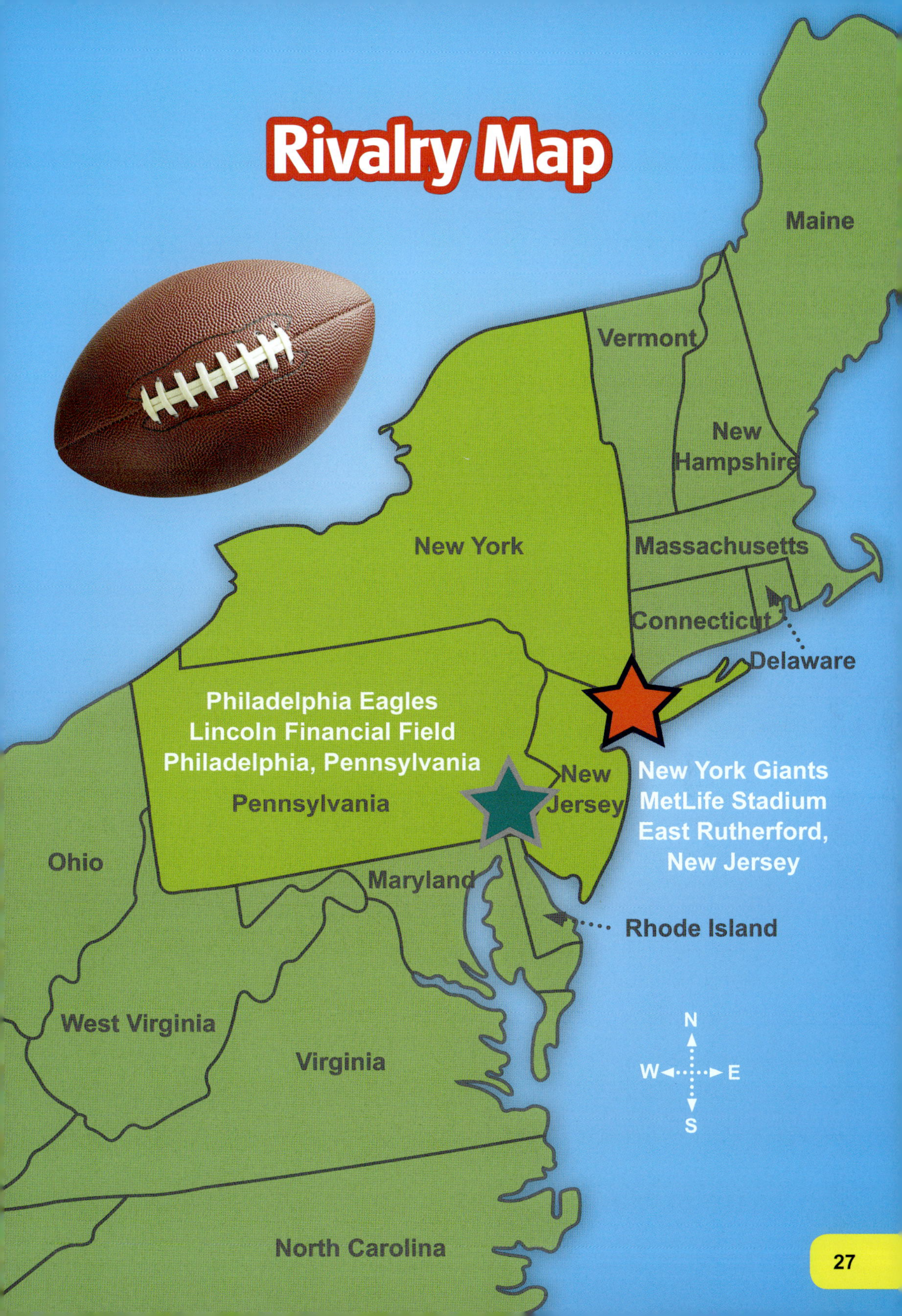
Maine
Vermont
New Hampshire
New York
Massachusetts
Connecticut
Delaware
Philadelphia Eagles
Lincoln Financial Field
Philadelphia, Pennsylvania
Pennsylvania
New Jersey
New York Giants
MetLife Stadium
East Rutherford,
New Jersey
Ohio
Maryland
Rhode Island
West Virginia
Virginia
N
W
E
S
North Carolina

BEYOND

THE BOOK

After reading the book, it's time to think about what you learned. Try the following exercises to jumpstart your ideas.

THINK

THAT'S NEWS TO ME. The 2017 Eagles won the Super Bowl. Find news sources about this game. What kinds of news sources will you look for? Where will you find them? What information could you learn?

CREATE

SHARPEN YOUR RESEARCH SKILLS. This book is about the Eagles–Giants rivalry. Find more information about the rivalry. Where could you go to find this information? Create a research plan. Think about the steps you will take. Then write a paragraph describing your plan. Include your next steps.

SHARE

SUM IT UP. Write a one paragraph summary of the book. Include all its key points. Write in your own words. Find a classmate. Show your classmate your paragraph. Ask him or her for feedback. Did you get all the key points? Did you miss anything? Does your classmate have any questions?

GROW

REAL-LIFE RESEARCH. Reading can tell you a lot about a topic. However, you can also learn a lot by experiencing something in person. Where would you go to learn more about Eli Manning or Donovan McNabb? What other things could you learn there?

RESEARCH NINJA

Visit www.ninjaresearcher.com/0813 to learn how to take your research skills and book report writing to the next level!

RESEARCH

DIGITAL LITERACY TOOLS

SEARCH LIKE A PRO
Learn about how to use search engines to find useful websites.

FACT OR FAKE?
Discover how you can tell a trusted website from an untrustworthy resource.

TEXT DETECTIVE
Explore how to zero in on the information you need most.

SHOW YOUR WORK
Research responsibly—learn how to cite sources.

WRITE

GET TO THE POINT
Learn how to express your main ideas.

PLAN OF ATTACK
Learn prewriting exercises and create an outline.

DOWNLOADABLE REPORT FORMS

Further Resources

BOOKS

Mack, Larry. *The New York Giants Story.* Bellwether Media, 2017.

Mack, Larry. *The Philadelphia Eagles Story*. Bellwether Media, 2017.

Scheff, Matt. *Incredible Football Records*. The Child's World, 2016.

WEBSITES

FACTSURFER

Factsurfer.com gives you a safe, fun way to find more information.

1. Go to www.factsurfer.com.
2. Enter "Eagles vs. Giants" into the search box and click 🔍.
3. Select your book cover to see a list of related websites.

Glossary

cornerback: The cornerback is a player who defends wide receivers. The Eagles receivers had trouble against the Giants cornerbacks.

defensive end: A defensive end is a player who starts each play on the edge of the defensive line. The defensive end chased down the quarterback.

fullback: The fullback is an offensive player who sometimes runs with the ball and often helps by blocking. The fullback ran through the offensive line and into the end zone.

halfback: The halfback is an offensive player who often runs with the ball out of the backfield. The halfback took the handoff and raced around the offensive line.

regulation: Regulation is play that occurs during regular game time. Each NFL game has four fifteen-minute quarters of regulation play.

sack: A sack is when the quarterback is tackled before he gets to pass the ball. Michael Strahan broke through the offensive line to record a sack.

ticker tape parade: Ticker tape parades honor local heroes and are famous for people throwing confetti onto the parade route. New York City celebrated the Giants' Super Bowl win with a ticker tape parade.

Index

PHOTO CREDITS

The images in this book are reproduced through the courtesy of: Tony Gutierrez/AP Images, front cover (left); Damian Strohmeyer/AP Images, front cover (right); EFKS/Shutterstock Images, front cover (background); dean bertoncelj/Shutterstock Images, p. 3 (left); Jeff Bukowski/Shutterstock Images, p. 3 (right); Richard Cavalleri/Shutterstock Images, p. 4; Kathy Willens/AP Images, pp. 5, 6; Red Line Editorial, pp. 7, 27 (chart); Bill Kostroun/AP Images, pp. 8–9; AP Images, pp. 10–11; Harry Harris/AP Images, p. 12; enterlinedesign/Shutterstock Images, p. 13; Evan Pinkus/AP Images, pp. 14–15, 22; Peter Morgan/AP Images, pp. 16–17; Henny Ray Abrams/AP Images, p. 18; JStone/Shutterstock Images, p. 20; Al Messerschmidt/AP Images, p. 21; Bill Raymond/Shutterstock Images, p. 23; Alex Brandon/AP Images, p. 24 (crowd); Al Tielemans/AP Images, p. 25 (mask); Mark Lennihan/AP Images, p. 26; MG SG/Shutterstock Images, 27 (football); Ken Durden/Shutterstock Images, p. 30.

ABOUT THE AUTHOR

Carrie Myers lives in New York City with her husband, three children, and one very hairy guinea pig. She enjoys music, books, and visiting family in Hawaii. She does not enjoy washing dishes.